SECURING YOUR MARITAL DESTINY

No More Marital Delay

Joe-Jesimiel Ogbe

SECURING YOUR MARITAL DESTINY

All scripture quotations are from the King James Version of the Bible, except otherwise stated.

ISBN: 978-978-55429-0-5

Published in Nigeria by:

YOUNG DISCIPLES PRESS

Printed In Nigeria by:

Livingproof Press Limited

1, Heal The World Avenue, Opposite Shoprite, Sango Ota, Ogun State.

For further information or permission, contact:

DIRECTOR OF PUBLICATIONS,

Young Disciples International (Ydi)

3, YDI Street off Isheri-LASU Road (By Hotel Solous B/Stop), Igando, Lagos

Tel: 01-2934286, 08023124455

E-mail: joejesimiel2006@yahoo.com

www.ydiworld.org

Contents

DEDICATION

To Late Pastor (Mrs) Bimbo Odukoya

Who served God as one of the foremost pioneers in singles ministry in Nigeria via her impactful seminars, books and TV program!

INTRODUCTION

For quite some time now I have been eminently concerned about the state of mature singles in our churches! I'm concerned because many of them are hurting! Many are even frustrated to the point of jettisoning the idea of getting married completely. Having been in the trenches of youth and singles ministry for over three decades, I can understand and attest to the pain and trauma they go through.

The plain truth is that marital delays are real! Relationship challenges are real! But equally real is the power of God to frustrate, shatter and scatter such delays and challenges. For we have an assurance that through the greatness of God's power, our enemies shall submit themselves to us! Marital Delays shall submit to you this time around.

My dear single, have you wondered why some relationships are not working or experiencing a headway as they should? Have you wondered why so many relationships these days are plagued with a

1

plethora of heartbreaks, disappointments, breakups and what have you? The devil, enemy of the marriage institution is at work! He has kept many lovely singles under his wicked lock and key! The wicked enemy has marshaled out spiritual forces to thwart their great marital destinies. No wonder, even no matter how rich, handsome or beautiful they may be, they still find it difficult to realize their marital desires! What a shame!

I have seen and ministered to some single ladies who were tormented by spiritual husbands! These evil forces have stopped potential husbands from looking at them for any serious relationship. The devil has made them look ugly and unattractive, even though they were good looking and attractive physically! What a wicked devil, you would say!

Are you tormented by the devil in this regard?

Be rest assured, your freedom is finally here! God has assured me that He will use this book to deliver millions of singles from the shackles of the devil and self-inflicted bondages. As God's instrument of deliverance, I hereby invoke the superior power of God to shatter and defeat the host of the enemy in your life. I decree that by the power of God, your unattractive personality is hereby changed to an attractive personality! I forcefully remove every evil veil the devil and his cohorts have covered your marital destiny with. By the blood of Jesus, I secure your colorful marital destiny. Your God ordained spouse will locate you forthwith in Jesus name!

Israelites were ordained and destined by God to take delivery of their promised land but they needed to confront, fight and defeat their enemies that stood in their way before they could enjoy the land flowing with milk and honey. Do you want to enjoy the milk and honey of marriage? Then you must be prepared to confront and fight every enemy that stands in your way to securing your marital destiny. No single secures his or her marital possession or destiny by wishing! As we all know that no champion wins a contest on a platter of gold! Every champion contends ferociously with his opponent to win the gold medal!

Finally, the book that will aid you in fighting and winning the war against marital delays and relationship challenges is here! In this compact but powerful book, I'm inspired to give you power instruments that will guarantee your victory, if you dare to engage them in faith. You shall no longer be burdened with issues of delay anymore. With knowledge of your rights and privileges as a child of God you shall obtain your heart's desire in no distant future. I can assure you that God who did it for others will also do it for you as He is no respecter of persons.

I have proofs - testimonies cum true life stories of individuals that God turned their marital captivity. The Bible says, "When the LORD turned again the captivity of Zion, we were like them that dream." You too shall experience a captivity turning power of God and your anticipated desire or long held dream of getting married shall be fully realized! If you are truly born again, God's thoughts or plans for you are good and splendid! He has determined to bring you to an expected end as far as the issue of marriage is concerned. "For I know the thoughts that I think toward you, saith the LORD, thoughts of peace, and not of evil, to give you an expected end." (Jer 29:11)

Even if you missed it in your first attempt at marriage, God of second chance, will give you a fresh start. Don't be despondent! God who gave one of my young disciples at Ydi a second chance, will do same for you. (See the Appendix and read her story)

Please understand that the God who said, "It is not good for a man to be alone" will settle you maritally! You need faith! You need knowledge! You need to know how to "go to the city" of a blissful marriage!

The Bible says, "The labour of the foolish wearieth every one of them, because he knoweth not how to go to the city." (Ecclesiastes 10:15)

With knowledge which you will be acquainted with via this book, you will no longer be stranded in your journey toward a blissful marriage. Knowledge is power! Knowing what to do is important but doing what you know is superior. Mary the mother of our Lord Jesus said, "whatever He tells you to do, do it!" It is in your doing that you secure your miracle. It is in your embracing and carrying out the instructions that you are blessed! My candid prayer for you is that you will be meek and humble enough to accept and carry out my God-inspired instructions, for they are meant to aid the procurement of your marital destiny.

Happy Reading!

Joe jesimiel Ogbe

October, 2017

1 REASONS FOR DELAYED OR NO MARRIAGE

There are legions of reasons why many mature singles are experiencing delayed or no marriage. Some singles are single because of involuntary or voluntary reasons. Voluntarily, some have made up their minds not to get married at all for some personal or religious reasons. For such singles, I cannot help them! But if your case is involuntary, then this chapter might be an eye opener for you! Below are ten vital and proven reasons why many singles are unmarried today:

1. The Enemy at Work

The devil, like I stated in the introduction of this book, is the enemy of the marriage institution. This enemy fights and manipulates ferociously many lovely singles. He has kept many of them under his wicked lock and key, refusing them to enjoy blissful marriage. He is the power or force behind spiritual husbands. He is the one behind every evil or wicked generational curses that have thwarted great marital destinies. The devil is not a gentleman! No! Not at all! He does not play gentle with anyone. If given the chance or opportunity he will steal, kill or destroy, as this is his ministry! The Bible says, "The thief cometh not, but for to steal, and to kill, and to destroy: I am come that they might have life, and that they might have it more abundantly." (John 10:10)

Believe me, the devil is walking up and down, attacking many singles today with depression, fear, pride, lusts, disappointments, separation; and all those nasty, defeatist thoughts that come into their minds. He is behind so many evil family patterns! For instance, in some families, the devil has determined and ordered that their first born sons and daughters will experience delayed or no marriage at all. He has become a major force determining the marital destiny of many singles. But he will not succeed in your life in Jesus mighty name! Your own case shall be different!

If you know your enemy and his strategy of attack or warfare, you are most likely going to defeat him!

God has enabled me to package some power instruments that will help you to defeat him finally! (Check out these instruments in chapter seven!)

2. Sickness or Illness

Sickness or illness is a robber of marital destiny.

A single who is plagued or bedeviled with one sickness or the other cannot think or talk of marriage. Marriage can never be a consideration if the sickness troubling them is chronic. I know some singles who are scared to consider marriage because they know that their illness could disqualify them. One major issue chronically ill people face in finding love is disclosure. The question of when to tell a prospective partner about their health status or condition can be very disturbing. Sharing information too soon may even scare a prospective partner off and sharing too late may lead to a lack of trust. What a state of dilemma!

One of my relations died of HIV/AIDS! We believe she contracted the deadly virus from her randy husband. If the man had disclosed his HIV status to her, she would not have gone ahead with the marriage. There's no known cure for this disease, hence it's a height of wickedness not disclosing one's HIV status to someone you profess to love.

Why should you be the one spreading the virus to other people? How can you go out with someone and not tell the person about your health condition?

Come out clear and clean about your health status, if he or she loves you beyond your condition, that's splendid. But by all means, don't be deceptive and think that all will be okay after you get married. May I also chip in that you don't have to jump into bed with someone whose health condition you're not sure off. You might end up contracting a very terrible disease.

3. Unattractive Personality

Unattractive personality is one reason why so many singles fail to get married on time. Some singles have no inviting, pleasing, appealing or beneficial features. Their personalities repel rather than attract. There is more to your personality than your personal appearance. Please know that no one, and this includes you, is born with a pleasing personality. An attractive or pleasing personality must be consciously cultivated through social interaction. Many singles don't have a social life at all! Some are not affable. You become an affable person by choice! Affability is a quality of being approachable. Are you difficult to be approached? An affable single is a person who is not difficult to approach or talk to, because of his or her polite and friendly disposition.

Every single who truly desires to settle down must embrace a cheerful disposition. Gloom and depression not only take much out of life, but detract greatly from your chances of finding love. Does your facial expression radiate the fact that you are not friendly? Unfriendly face, looking or acting miserable certainly will not attract people to you.

I recently ministered to a mature lady who desperately wanted to settle down, but discovered to my chagrin that this lady never had the superior art of conversation at all. She talked too much about herself, her achievements, her beauty and other ephemeral things. She even boasted about what she's done for her siblings. As far as I'm concerned a single who makes herself or himself the principal object of conversation will rebuff prospective partners. Be a good listener, instead of being a braggart talker!

I got attracted to my wife via her sterling qualities of courtesy and politeness. She puts up such moral excellence of exquisite tenderness, conducive for a robust relationship, which compelled me to ask her out. A friendly smile will go a long way in expressing your true and pure personality.

4. Self Centeredness

If "Self " is at the center of your existence, it might be pretty difficult for you to secure your marital destiny.

Many singles are preoccupied with themselves! What a shame! They are not benevolent. They don't have the desire to do good for others. They don't engage in sharing or giving to others. If you want to secure your marital destiny, deliberately and concertedly jettison the idea or lifestyle of selfishness!

Rebekah got her future husband via her benevolence. She went the extra mile to help a stranger who later turned out to be a go between her and Isaac, her future husband. The Bible says, "And she said, Drink, my lord: and she hasted, and let down her pitcher upon her hand, and gave him drink. And when she had done giving him drink, she said, I will draw water for thy camels also, until they have done drinking. And she hasted, and emptied her pitcher into the trough, and ran again unto the well to draw water, and drew for all his camels." (Genesis 24:18-20)

5. Rejection

Many singles that have been rejected or jilted in the past find it hard to start a new relationship, hence delayed marriage! In order to prevent further hurts they begin to suspect the intentions of intending partners. They have the suspicion or fear that their next relationship maybe worse.

Do you have the lethargy to start a new relationship?

Have you embraced self-rejection, and begin to think you are the reason why suitors are not coming? Maybe you are feeling insecure, and even practically you have no confidence in yourself, you judge yourself as being less qualified to enter into a thriving relationship. Don't worry! God who used me to deliver a beloved sister who was a victim of sexual abuse will deliver you too! This sister found it difficult to trust men, until I ministered to her and delivered her from the mental and emotional trauma of abuse. I ministered to her and set her free from the spirit of bitterness which had made her unwilling to forgive or let go of her past. I told her in clear terms that bitterness is an evil fruit produced by her unwillingness to forgive her abuser, and that as a believer she is required to forgive the person who has hurt her. We are enjoined not to be defiled by bitterness! The Bible says, "Looking diligently lest any man fail of the grace of God; lest any root of bitterness springing up trouble you, and thereby many be defiled;" (Hebrew 12:15)

Have you ever been refused or turned down?

Have you been rebuffed or avoided like a leper?

Have you been shunned, neglected or even ignored as if you are a nobody? Then arise ferociously and deal with rejection right now! You cannot secure your marital destiny until you reject every form of rejection! Don't get into Self-Pity! Self-pity is an inward reaction to rejection. Self-pity is a form of Self-affliction whereby you permit yourself to indulge in thoughts of unfairness until you become thoroughly miserable. It is a practice guaranteed to destroy joy and peace, two of the precious fruits of the Holy Spirit!

One of the sisters who suffered the plague of delayed marriage was actually molested by inferiority complex. Inferiority is closely related to rejection. This sister was put down by her mother who never saw anything good in her. She eventually joined her mother to put herself down. Her mother compared her with her siblings from when she was a kid. She saw herself from the eyes or views of her mother, and began to evaluate herself as inferior.

It's not good to compare yourself with anybody. You are not wise if you do so! The Bible says, "For we dare not make ourselves of the number, or compare ourselves with some that commend themselves: but they measuring themselves by themselves, and comparing themselves among themselves, are not wise." (2 cor 10:12)

In God's sight no man or woman is inferior! Place value on yourself!

6. Hopelessness

A single who sees no prospect of being married is like a man trapped in Sahara desert with nothing but kilometres of hot sand in all direction. His tongue becomes swollen with thirst, he falls on the desert floor awaiting death. He is utterly hopeless! Without hope there is no joy, without joy there is no desire to attempt or venture into a new relationship.

Wrong reactions to the hurts of the past make bad matters worse. Learn to handle your past or current hurts scripturally. Why? Even our Lord Jesus was despised and rejected of men, yet , He did not end up with a disintegrated personality. When you walk in His steps, you will obtain the same results. When you handle your hurts wrongly, there will be repercussions. God forbid that you should contemplate pouring acid on your Ex who jilted you! It's wrong to avenge wrongs done to you! It's right and biblical to forgive people.

Only God has remedy for hurts and hopelessness!

Only God of hope can fill your heart with joy and peace in the expectation of your wedding day!

Only God can cause you to abound in hope via the power of the Holy Spirit. "Now the God of hope fill you with all joy and peace in believing, that ye may abound in hope, through the power of the Holy Ghost." (Romans 15:13)

7. Disheveled Appearance

Candidly, some singles are experiencing delayed marriage simply because of their disheveled appearance! How can you have the habit of disheveled appearance or being unkempt and expect to find a partner? It is a fallacy to think that your appearance is not a factor. I'm of firm conviction that your appearance is equally important as your character and spirituality. Before Joseph appeared before an earthly king, Pharaoh, he had to shave himself and change his garment. Joseph had a change of garment to validate his change of status – prison to palace.

As a single, your appearance or dressing matters to a large extent. Your dressing is very important, because people see your container before your content! Joseph dressed for the palace to create the atmosphere of acceptance. You too can dress to create the atmosphere of acceptance! You needed to see me on the day I proposed to my wife! It was as if I was going for a job interview. I was not casual! I dressed to create an atmosphere of respect. A good prayer life and Bible study life are excellent and important, but packaging yourself is equally important. Many singles require urgent personal hygiene grooming if they truly desire to secure their marital destiny. You can have a brilliant mind and have a bad breath. Body odour is not a mark of spirituality or holiness!

Bachelors! Please be neat and do keep a low cut.

Your hair must not be bushy! Do a haircut quite often. Shave your beard often. Develop the habit of using good deodorant and cologne (perfume) that is compatible with your body. Keep your shoes shined at all times. Your socks must be fresh. Take care of your clothes and always wear clean clothes. Your inner wears require more attention! Your dressing must make a statement of a serious minded gentleman, not an unserious Casanova!

Spinsters! Never dress seductively. Opening or exposing your cleavages will not attract you to serious minded suitors. You will only be attracted to playboys. Excessive jewelry and make up are not ideal for wife materials! Don't "paint" yourself or make up like Jezebel.

There is beauty in simplicity!

There is beauty in being natural!

8. Character Defects

Largely, many singles are experiencing delayed marriage simply because of their character defects! It can be said that a "character defect" is a behavior, habit, or attitude that causes recurring negative consequences for you or the people around you.

Are you a chronic liar? Do you have problem with stealing, infidelity, irresponsibility, anger and unreliability? Then you have a defective character!

You may not always see your defects for what they are, except lovely people around you tell you about them. Being aware of your faulty character and being willing to work on it will require humility.

Many singles are not willing and prepared to come face to face with their less attractive qualities. Please know that none of us can change our character defects until we become aware of them. Once we identify our defects, we will be able to see them more clearly and see how they affect us and the people around us.

Once we have a better handle on our strengths, we will have the balance that leads to true humility. Then, we can make a beginning of working on the solution.

Your appearance matters, but it's not all you need to secure your marital destiny! Your beauty or handsome physique is a gift from God, it can be harnessed to attract potential spouses, but what keeps him or her glued to you is your character.

Do you have a poor character?

Have people around you complained about your faulty character? Then arise assiduously as a matter of urgency to work toward robust character building, as men and women of character are not born, but made. We have too few singles of character today, because too few of them are willing to build their character. Don't focus too much on superficial things and self-importance. Rather focus on your personal character early and often. It is your character that will stand the test of time, not your beauty or position in society. (For more depths on character building, see chapter four!)

9. Lack of Money

Lack of money is a major reason why some chronic bachelors are not settled maritally. As we all know that money is the fuel of any given project! Money answers all things, and this includes marriage. The Bible says, "... but money answereth all things." (Ecclesiastes 10:19)

I advise that spinsters should consider praying for their potential husbands who are struggling to find a means of livelihood. Many potential husbands are still in the labour market searching for jobs! No man is prepared to carry an extra burden of fending for a wife if he does not have a job that guarantees regular income and happiness. Martin Luther King said, "If a man doesn't have a job or an income, he has neither life nor liberty, possibility for the pursuit of happiness. He merely exists."

It's a tragedy that many of our mature bachelors are merely existing. What a shame!

My beloved spinster, if you are privileged to have a partner who does not have much cash, your dream of getting married early may be marred, if you are the demanding type. It is not wise to place extra loads on your partner. I mean extra load of asking him to do some things for you or your parents before marriage. A couple of years ago, a brother called me on phone asking whether it was wise of his fiancé to insist that he must build a house for her retired dad in the village before their wedding. He was actually considering quitting the marriage completely. Many singles have foolishly frustrated their chances of getting married early. What a pity!

In some parts of Nigeria, bachelors are becoming extremely scared of venturing into the marriage institution due to marriage or wedding cost, especially high bride price. Ladies! Be wise! Don't allow your parents to frustrate your marital destiny through exorbitant bride price. You're not for sale!

Marriage is partnership! As such, two of you must learn and be prepared to share the burden of wedding cost. Instead of feeding the whole community, why not consider a low key wedding. I have even advised singles in our church to consider "church-blessing" instead of high society wedding.

While lack of money could hamper a bachelor's chances of getting married early, much money could hamper a spinster's chances of early marriage. I know a lady who allowed her money to "enter her head". She was in the habit of talking proudly: "I cannot submit to any man who is not richer than me." With all the prayers and prophetic declarations from great men of God she is still not married. Her attitude toward money must change if she really wants to settle down maritally. Beloved single, if your money is a blessing from God, it should not stultify your marital destiny or procure you sorrow. My Bible says, "The blessing of the LORD, it maketh rich, and he addeth no sorrow with it." (Proverbs 10:22)

10. Parental Interference

It will surprise you to know that not many parents are keen about their children getting married early.

I heard of a father who frustrated his daughter's marriage just because he felt his daughter would no longer support him financially. It took a spiritual warfare before his daughter got married. What about a mother who even vowed that over her death will her daughter be married. What a wicked mother you would say. Many parents are giving flimsy reasons or excuses why they will not allow their children to settle down early! Can you imagine a parent insisting that her daughter or son must marry from a particular race or tribe. A particular sister in our church is suffering from her father's tribalism. I pray she secures her freedom before it's too late!

Some parents have even become tools in the hands of the devil via proclamation of curses and even witchcraft, as they have been manipulating their children's destinies. How do I deal with a difficult or manipulative parent, you may ask? My response is that you must be wise. Never be foolish. Don't be confrontational. Engage in diplomacy. Give your father or mother a venison. A venison is anything your parents love that might provoke them to bless you. "Bring me venison, and make me savoury meat, that I may eat, and bless thee before the LORD before my death." (Genesis 27:7)

As a daughter you should know what your parents like. Shower them with gifts. But most importantly assure them that marriage will not stop your love or support to them.

In case, your parents prove difficult, intransigent or are not prepared to agree with you, don't worry, just commit them into the hands of the Lord. God has the power to turn their heart to be favorably disposed toward you. "The king's heart is in the hand of the LORD, as the rivers of water: he turneth it whithersoever he will." (Proverbs 21:1)

2 KNOWING HOW TO UNVEIL GOD'S SECRETS

In chapter one I tried to adduce some reasons why so many singles are still unmarried. The reasons given are not exhaustive! Only God has the perfect knowledge why singles who are ready and prepared for marriage still fall short of their expectation or desire!

Securing your marital destiny is not free! There is a price tag on it. It is therefore your onus to position yourself to do what is needful to possess your possession. What to do? Ask God to help you unveil or reveal the secrets behind your late marriage. The Bible says, "The secret things belong unto the LORD our God: but those things which are revealed belong unto us and to our children for ever, that we may do all the words of this law." (Deuteronomy 29:29)

Heavenly secrets are God's exclusive preserve. And until He reveals the secrets, they don't belong unto you.

God treasures concealing a matter!

It is His glory to conceal a matter, and it is your honor to search it out. The Bible says, "It is the glory of God to conceal a thing: but the honour of kings is to search out a matter." (Proverbs 25:2)

Your success in finding a partner is tied to your discovery of the secret behind your delayed marriage. Accept the truth that you knowing how to unveil god's secrets don't know what is responsible for your late marriage or why no suitor is coming your way. Accept the responsibility to call upon the Lord and He will show you what you don't know. The Bible says, "Call unto me, and I will answer thee, and shew thee great and mighty things, which thou knowest not." (Jeremiah 33:3)

A beloved sister used this scripture to pray, asking or demanding that God may show her the true picture of a particular brother who was asking her out, because she perceived that their relationship was shrouded with lots of secrecies. Not too long, God the Revealer of deep things showed her this brother's lifestyle of deception and pharisaical tendencies. The sister confronted him with her revelations and he got offended and disappeared into oblivion. These days many so called brothers and sisters in church are not transparent and truthful, only God can reveal the genuineness of their intentions or proposals.

Are there requirements for unveiling God's Secrets? Yes of course! Now let's take a look at the following four major requirements:

1. A Prayer of Enquiry Requirement

David never lost a single battle! Why? Because he always consulted or enquired of God. David was a man who never embarked on any task until he got a clear signal from God. The Bible says, "And David enquired at the LORD, saying, Shall I pursue after this troop? shall I overtake them? And he answered him, Pursue: for thou shalt surely overtake them, and without fail recover all." (1 Samuel 30:8)

Daniel and his friends, Hananiah, Mishael, and Azariah, passionately sought the mercies of the God of heaven concerning the demand of the king so that they might not perish with the rest of the wise men of Babylon. And God revealed the secrets to Daniel. The Bible says, "Then was the secret revealed unto Daniel in a night vision. Then Daniel blessed the God of heaven. Daniel answered and said, Blessed be the name of God for ever and ever: for wisdom and might are his: And he changeth the times and the seasons: he removeth kings, and setteth up kings: he giveth wisdom unto the wise, and knowledge to them that know understanding: He revealeth the deep and secret things: he knoweth what is in the darkness, and the light dwelleth with him." (Daniel 2:19-22)

Just as David, Daniel and co went to God in a prayer of enquiry, you too need to go before God in heartfelt prayers, asking Him to reveal to you reasons why you are still unmarried.

Pray thus: "Father God, All things lay bare before you, show me where I'm missing it in my quest to settling down. Father, what must I do to effect a change in the right direction? What must I do to experience or secure my marital destiny? Oh Lord kindly show me, I'm prepared to do whatever you reveal to me to do."

My Beloved single, you have a role to play. Be willing to do anything revealed to you.

"Then was the secret revealed unto Daniel." God has not changed. What He did for Daniel He will do for you too. If you can engage the prayer of enquiry like Daniel you too will have access to secrets of God.

My beloved single, one single secret from heaven is worth much more than a lifetime of efforts and struggles. One secret is enough to shatter your delayed or late marriage syndrome.

2. A search Requirement

The Bible is full of divine secrets or mysteries!

Don't be surprised to encounter some relevant insights from God's Word that will shatter your marital delays! I urge you therefore to prayerfully and deliberately go on a search into the Word with a view to connecting with a "sent word" that will help you take delivery of your marital portion. I believe there is a particular word for every challenge we face as God's children! As you study or search the Bible, ask God to open your eyes to locate His sent word that is apt for your condition or situation. God has not designed you for marital stagnation or retrogression. No! One revealed word from Him via the Bible, is powerful enough to secure your marital destiny.

Anointed books, like the one you are reading is loaded with insights, principles and testimonies which could procure your marital blessings!

For instance, this book is loaded with true life stories or testimonies of singles that have experienced what you are longing to experience right now. There are steps they have taken that secured their desires. Will you be humble enough to follow their steps? If you can do what they did to secure their marital destiny, you too may secure yours. Apostle Paul said, "Those things, which ye have both learned, and received, and heard, and seen in me, do: and the God of peace shall be with you." (Phil 4:9)

3. Love Requirement

God has packages of blessings for those that love Him. The Bible says, "But as it is written, Eye hath not seen, nor ear heard, neither have entered into the heart of man, the things which God hath prepared for them that love him." (1Cor. 2:9)

I do believe also that God will reveal His secrets to you if you truly love Him, as true love grants access to

God's secrets! Your love for God is what determines how much of His secrets you have access to or what He reveals to you. God has reserved packages for His lovers, so when you are able to win His love, He releases them unto you. One of such packages is having a blissful marriage!

Do you really love God? Be sincere! May be you are "lusting" after God, and thinking that you are loving Him. You "lust" after God if you are seeking Him to satisfy your whims and caprices! You "lust" after God, if you are using Him to satisfy your marital desire and then to later dump Him! Will you still love or serve Him as you used to do? Will you be this passionate about Him and His kingdom, going to church frequently if you are married? Will you not be giving excuses why you are no more available for God and His kingdom?

To love God is to worship and praise Him personally, privately and publicly. Decide today to worship and praise Him from your heart to demonstrate your love for Him. By all means try to put Him first. The number one commandment is to love God "with all your heart and with all your soul and with all your mind and with all your strength" It's an undivided love. God should be your topmost priority. If you love God with all your heart, soul, mind and strength, then you won't allow other things such as your job or friends to crowd in. And most importantly, to love God is to desire Him, to yearn or pant after Him!

"As the deer pants for streams of water, so my soul pants for you, O God" (Psalm 42:1)

You can't pant after God, and He will not pant after you!

It will interest you to know that as a lover of God, all things are designed by Him to work together for your good. The Bible says, "And we know that all things work together for good to them that love God, to them who are the called according to his purpose." (Romans 8:28)

Maybe even your current seemingly lack of partner will work out for your good. How? God might be reserving you for His beloved son! He will soon orchestrate this "perfect" partner into your life. Someone who will love and be there for you 24/7!

Don't forget, a patient dog eats the fattest bone!

Be patient, God is at work in your favor! Some years ago a beloved daughter of Zion who felt she had waited long enough for a partner but to no avail came to see me for prayers. In a seriously traumatized voice, she told me how no serious guy had asked her out and how she felt abnormal.

I simply opened my mouth and declared: "God has reserved you for His VIP son. God will soon reveal him to you!" To God be all the glory, not too long after my prophetic declaration, a handsome brother who was serving as a special Assistant to a Governor emerged from the blues and proposed marriage to this lady. Today, they are happily married with wonderful children.

You are next inline!

Only believe!

4. Fear of God Requirement

God reveals His secrets to those that fear Him!

The Bible says, "The secret of the LORD is with them that fear him; and he will shew them his covenant." (Psalm 25:14)

Are you a God fearing single? Then be rest assured that God will unveil or reveal those secrets you need to know about those agents of the devil working assiduously against your marital destiny. I decree that your spiritual or inner eyes be opened to see what is standing on your way to a blissful marriage. My God, the Revealer of secrets, will reveal through dreams and visions all the secrets you need to secure your marital destiny. My God will work against all those people and places working against your marital destiny. Oh God, my heavenly Father arise and reveal the secrets behind the delayed or no marriage of your beloved son/daughter who fears You forthwith in Jesus' mighty name! Amen!

3 MARRIAGE INDUCING ATTITUDE

Attitude is a mindset or a tendency to respond positively or negatively towards a certain idea, object, person, or situation. Attitude is a predisposition or a settled way of thinking that provokes a certain behavior or action. Many singles hold different kinds of attitudes about marriage. Some Negative, some Positive! Some energy sapping, some energy energizing! Some marriage inducing, some marriage dissuading!

Believe it or not, your attitude has the capacity to secure your marital destiny or discourage you from getting married.

My goal in this chapter is to help you cultivate a marriage inducing attitude. Even if you have held a marriage discouraging attitude before now, there is hope for you! I'm confident that all the negative stories about marriage which have molded your attitude over the years can be jettisoned or discarded if you dare embrace my wise counsel.

Your marriage attitude does not emerge from what happens to you, but instead from how you decide to interpret what happens to you. Take, for example, if your mother had a failed marriage, you're most likely going to interpret marriage from your mother's experience and begin to develop a mindset or attitude that marriage is not a worthy venture. You might even move further to say some negative stuffs to yourself such as: "I don't think I'm caught out for marriage. I will not allow any man to maltreat me. All men are the same, if my father could maltreat my mum, there's no way that my husband will not maltreat me. I don't want to pass through what my mother passed through, no way!"

One of my cousins developed a very negative attitude about marriage because of her dysfunctional family. She was never keen on getting married at all. Thank God for using me to counsel and deliver her from the satanic bondage of negativity. Today, to the glory of God, she is happily married to a God-fearing man who loves her and her children. You don't share the same destiny or fingerprint with your mother or father. Except you allow it, through negative mindset, what befell your mother is not permitted to befall you! What befell your father will not befall you. The marital trauma you saw all around you while growing up cannot be your lot! This is the truth!

From the Word of God, you can fortify your mindset that you can't suffer or bear the iniquity of your father and mother! Even as they too will not bear yours. Your positive, right attitude or righteousness shall be upon you or your negative, wrong attitude or unrighteousness shall be upon you! It's all about your choice! The Bible says, "The word of the LORD came unto me again, saying, What mean ye, that ye use this proverb concerning the land of Israel, saying, The fathers have eaten sour grapes, and the children's teeth are set on edge? As I live, saith the Lord GOD, ye shall not have occasion any more to use this proverb in Israel. Behold, all souls are mine; as the soul of the father, so also the soul of the son is mine: the soul that sinneth, it shall die." (Ezekiel 18:1-4)

Accept Personal Responsibility

Accept personal responsibility to develop or cultivate right and positive attitude that attracts your potential partner to you. Deliberately jettison negative attitude that repels potential suitors or spouses. Your attitude is a major key to securing your marital destiny. In my work with singles for over 30 years I can truly declare that many are stranded in the journey toward their blissful marriage due to poor attitude. It's a negative attitude to see the worst aspect of your delayed marriage, or to believe that due to age factor you may not get married at all.

Change your attitude! For I have seen and heard of people in their 50s and 60s getting married. Lack of hope or confidence in your relationship is pessimism. Instead of dwelling on pessimism, dwell on optimism! While pessimism wears you down, optimism cheers you up. My beloved single, I'm confident about your relationship. I'm optimistic that you will get married in your due season! My Bible says, "He hath made every thing beautiful in his time..." (Ecclesiastes 3:11)

4 ways to engender Positive Attitude

1. Positive Words engender Positive Attitude

Always say good and positive things about marriage and married people, thereby engendering positive attitude! Never denigrate or castigate this honorable institution, for the Word of God, the Bible has good things to say about marriage: "Marriage is honourable in all, and the bed undefiled: but whoremongers and adulterers God will judge." (Hebrews 13:4)

"Let us be glad and rejoice, and give honour to him: for the marriage of the Lamb is come, and his wife hath made herself ready." (Revelation 19:7)

Don't forget! Jesus performed His first miracle during a marriage feast in Cana of Galilee. If marriage were to be bad or evil the righteous Son of a righteous God would not have been in attendance.

How do you respond or react to a statement like this from your partner: "Sorry we can't get along. I quit." You might respond aggressively with an abusive language or you might respond calmly by thanking him for how far both of you have come, appreciating him or her for the wonderful time both of you shared while the relationship lasted. Speaking abusively or cursing the person is negative! Choosing an edifying language is positive! If you want to have a positive attitude, your vocabulary must be consistently positive. Stop using negative phrases such as "I can't find a trustworthy partner." "It's impossible these days to find true love" or "I don't think this relationship will work." These type of statements program you for negative results.

Put out a positive attitude via positive words, and you'll have positive, joyful results. Put out a bad, negative attitude via negative words, and you'll have negative, bad results. Do you know that just as your beauty or physique is contagious, so is your attitude? You can be a source of positive energy or a source of negative energy to yourself through your words. With your words you can edify yourself and those around you. Don't join people who don't have anything good to say about marriage. I have seen many singles who are not enthusiastic about marriage at all! Some don't even feel good about anything. Marriage is a good institution! Treasure it. Feel good about it! From this moment, begin to say, speak, talk and declare good things that prove to God and man that you love to enter into this noble institution.

2. The Word of God Engender Positive Attitude

There is nothing that fortifies your positive attitude like the Word of God! I'm eternally encouraged, enthralled and enthusiastic about the word of God. Have you found the word fascinating before? Maybe you were at your lowest ebb emotionally but through the word you were refreshed, reenergized and revitalized. I'm of firm conviction that every born again child of God can develop a positive attitude about life. Why? Because God has got our back! His love and good plans for us are splendid. For goodness sake, who will say, you won't make it, when God has not said so? Who will say, you won't amount to anything, when God has not said so? Who has the right to say you will not marry, when God has not said so?

Even if you fail so many times, God will cause you to rise again!

Please say emphatically and prophetically:

"I will rise again!" It shall be unto you according to your faith and declaration!

You must believe that everything will work for your good. The Bible says, "And we know that all things work together for good to them that love God, to them who are the called according to his purpose." (Romans 8:28)

Develop the positive attitude that even if someone walks out of your life, a better person is coming into your life. It's a positive attitude to think that singleness is not a disadvantage or a curse.

To be cheerful at all times is to be positive.

Instead of telling yourself "There's no way this relationship will work," tell yourself, "This relationship will work by the help of God. I'm investing my time and resources to make it work. I shall not labour in vain. I shall not build this relationship and another enjoy it, no way!" The Bible says, "And they shall build houses, and inhabit them; and they shall plant vineyards, and eat the fruit of them. They shall not build, and another inhabit; they shall not plant, and another eat: for as the days of a tree are the days of my people, and mine elect shall long enjoy the work of their hands. They shall not labour in vain, nor bring forth for trouble; for they are the seed of the blessed of the LORD, and their offspring with them." (Isaiah 65:21-23)

3. Positive Thoughts Promote Positive Attitude

Where does negative attitude come from?

Majorly, it comes from your negative thoughts. When you think negative thoughts over and over, they become part of your subconscious being, part of your personality. Many singles don't even realize they have a negative attitude because it's been with them for so long. For instance, some singles always expect rejection, disappointment and breakups. And that expectation turns them into a magnet for rejection, disappointment and breakups.

You expect the worst, so you get the worst! You expect the best, so you get the best! You are the product of your thoughts! "For as he thinketh in his heart, so is he..." (Proverbs 23:7)

As a single you have a choice, to think evil or think good! You can choose that inner self-motivation, or you can choose one of self-defeat and self-pity. No doubt, it's possible that you have had hard times and emotional trauma due to your long wait for your partner. The key is to realize it's not what happens to you that matters; it's how you choose to respond. Someone said, "Your mind is a computer that can be programmed. You can choose whether the software installed is productive or unproductive. Your inner dialogue is the software that programs your attitude, which determines how you present yourself to the world around you. You have control over the programming. Whatever you put into it is reflected in what comes out."

Garbage in, garbage out!

4. Positive People Engender Positive Attitude

With all sense of modesty and responsibility, I am a relationship expert, having authored seven titles on relationships. The truth is that you may be unmarried today because of the influence of people in your life! At a very tender age, people have shaped your mentality subconsciously or consciously. If you have been surrounding yourself with negative people who never see anything good in marriage, you too will never see anything good or positive about getting married. I have ministered to many singles who have behavior patterns that were programmed into their brains while in the company of friends. The sad reality of life is that you will continue to hear negative statements, such as: "good partners have gone extinct, no human being can make you happy, men are all the same, they are a bunch of cheats."

The easiest way to engender Positive Attitude is to associate with positive people who see and talk positive stuffs all the time. Never allow negative people to stuff your brain with all the rubbish stuffs. Don't allow them to gain control of your most influential voice, I mean your own inner voice. The message you allow will work for or against you!

If a friend says, "good men have gone extinct" counter this message immediately in your mind that:

"my case is different. My own man has not gone extinct. God has prepared for me the best husband in town. He will soon manifest and I shall testify!"

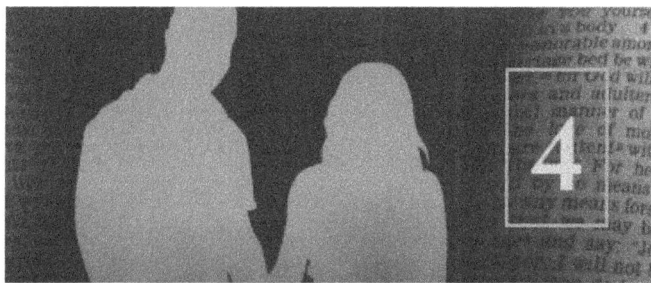

4 BUILDING A ROBUST CHARACTER

One way to build a robust character is to identify positive character templates, I mean people who exhibit desirable character traits. As a single, make it a goal to connect with such individuals. Spend time with them, talking with and learning from them. These templates should be individuals that you love to hang out with because you admire and want to be like them.

You don't build character by surrounding yourself with people who are bereft of character. Surround yourself with dishonest, unfaithful and uncultured people, soon you will like them! You are not immune to influence! Ruth built her robust character by following a character template in the person of Naomi. "And Ruth said, Intreat me not to leave thee, or to return from following after thee: for whither thou goest, I will go; and where thou lodgest, I will lodge: thy people shall be my people, and thy God my God: Where thou diest, will I die, and there will I be buried: the LORD do so to me, and more also, if ought but death part thee and me." (Ruth 1:16-17)

It takes positive character to be selfless. Ruth was selfless. It takes selflessness to follow an old woman who does not have the chance of giving birth to a son! Selflessness is having too much concern about other people's welfareto the detriment of yours. Ruth incarnated or embodied this character quality! Singles that display this character trait of selflessness will never lack partner to settle down with!

Character building is about developing convictions

To build character you must develop strong convictions or beliefs on your core values or important issues of life. What are your core values as a person? What are those things you will never do no matter the pressure? Do you have convictions about what is right or wrong? As a growing up teen, I had developed the conviction that divorce was not going to be an option for me no matter the marital challenge I may be confronted with. Today, to the glory of God,

I have been married for over 27 years without a thought or consideration of divorce!

You should be a man or a woman of principles and convictions!

Nelson Mandela said, "For anybody which changes his principles depending on whom he is dealing with, that is not a man who can lead a nation."

I like to add that any single who changes his principles like a chameleon is not fit for marriage institution. Personally, I don't have respect for singles who can always be swayed, or those who are neither here nor there and those who are "wishy- washy"! I don't have respect for Christian Singles who go about sleeping with prospective partners in the hope that premarital sex would cement their union. What a shame! Stand with your godly principles and convictions even if you stand alone.

Character building is about Self improvement

Building character is an essential part of lifelong learning. If you want to be a single that other people will look up to for inspiration, someone that they would readily recommend for serious relationship, try to make an active effort to improve yourself day in, day out. Take practical steps toward self improvement. A beloved daughter in the Lord sold her phone to attend a seminar with a view to improving herself, and a co-participant in the seminar introduced her to his friend for a serious relationship. Find avenues or opportunities for self improvement. Improve yourself in the area of skill acquisition. Learn to cook some dishes which you're not familiar with. Learn new languages and what have you.

Character building is about Attentiveness

Attentiveness is all about you showing the worth of a person or task by giving your undivided attention or concentration. Many singles these days do not give undivided attention to their relationships, they are simply "busy here and there"! No wonder they are not commanding quality results in their relationships.

It is a good character trait to welcome and give your partner undivided attention. Look into his or her eyes to show that he or she is worth your love and attention. It is a good, positive character to be focused on one partner per time.

It is a bad, negative character to keep multiple partners. No room for "spare tyre" relationships if you are a person of character.

Character building is about fortifying Integrity

You build your character when you consciously and deliberately fortify your integrity, when you choose to be a man or woman of truth, honesty and rectitude.

Today, many single ladies are longing to go out with God fearing and faithful men. But the truth is that faithful men are scarce to find. The Bible says, "Most men will proclaim every one his own goodness: but a faithful man who can find?" (Proverbs 20:6)

Integrity is a character trait that cements and sustains relationships.

Integrity is what keeps you faithful and loyal to your partner even if he or she is not in view. You fortify Integrity by allowing your words to match with your actions, and by staying faithful to your promises. Have you kept basic promises? You are a man of integrity if you keep your word. For instance, you promised your partner you will be at her place by 5pm, and by 4:30pm you are already waiting to be ushered in! Integrity is all about choosing that which is good instead of evil! As a Christian, having received the Spirit of Christ to know good from evil, you should always choose the good. "Butter and honey shall he eat, that he may know to refuse the evil, and choose the good." (Isaiah 7:15)

5 POWER OF THINKING AND IMAGINATION

Every single must wire himself or herself with the power of thinking and imagination, for with this power you can determine the direction of your marital destiny. With this power you can be married in a jiffy or you can stay long in the "market" of singleness, wishing someone will come to choose you.

Thinking in our context, is about your ability to direct your mind toward your prospective partner or marriage. It is your ability to actively use your mind to form connected ideas about your relationship; considering the possibility or impossibility of a course of action, such as thinking of becoming married or not. Imagination is all about you visualizing or forming images of a possible outcome.

Have you thought or imagined your wedding day?

My beloved spinster, if you can think, imagine and visualize when your father will walk you down the aisle to give you out in a holy matrimony; if you can begin right now to fantasize about your honeymoon in Dubai or Hawaii; if you can dare dream or visualize the kind of fun you will have with your spouse, surely those imaginations will become practical realities!

God respects and honors our imagination! He only disallows our self centered projects that do not bring Him glory. Whatever positive thing you have imagined to do or become, God will not frustrate but ensure its practical fulfillment. The Bible says, "And the LORD said, Behold, the people is one, and they have all one language; and this they begin to do: and now nothing will be restrained from them, which they have imagined to do." (Genesis 11:6)

Nelson Mandela has written extensively on how visualisation helped him maintain a positive attitude while being imprisoned for 27 years. He said, "I thought continually of the day when I would walk free. I fantasised about what I would like to do." Visualization works well to improve positive attitude.

To fortify your thinking or imagination, define big goals for yourself. Define the best possible wedding or marriage you are craving for, by drawing up a wedding or marriage plan. Move further by concretizing your plan by even buying kitchen utensils, such as plates which you want to use to serve your partner! Most of the utensils we used when we newly got married were bought by my wife as she was waiting for marriage.

Make no excuses, conceptualize your marriage or home right now. You can even start living in your dream home right away! It's not crazy to do that.

Do you have a dream of the kind of kids you want?

Do you have mental pictures or images of where you want to raise them? Is it in Nigeria? Then what part of Nigeria? Is it in Lagos? Then what kind of neighborhood? No excuse, aim for the best!

Go for it!

You are majorly a product of your thinking! The Bible says, "For as he thinketh in his heart, so is he ..." (Proverbs 23:7)

If you constantly think of being married, you will soon be married. And if you think about not getting married, maybe, due to shortage of good or best people to go out with, you are very much likely going to stay unmarried for a long while! Why? Because you have a very poor thinking pattern that robs you of your marital destiny.

God is not against you getting married to the best person out there! The Bible says, "This is the thing which the LORD doth command concerning the daughters of Zelophehad, saying, Let them marry to whom they think best; only to the family of the tribe of their father shall they marry." (Numbers 36:6)

How I wish you will form a mental image of getting married to the best spouse! Nothing will stop you from getting married or having the best! Not even the devil can stop the product of your imagination from manifesting!

6 ENGAGING THE POWER OF FAITH

"For though we walk in the flesh, we do not war after the flesh: For the weapons of our warfare are not carnal, but mighty through God to the pulling down of strong holds;" (2 Corinthians 10:3-4)

My beloved single, the enemy you have to war against is not physical, as such the use of physical weapons will not suffice. The only weapon you have is faith. "... this is the victory that overcometh the world, even our faith." (1 John 5:4)

Forces of darkness are real! Household enemies are real! If a mother could tie down the marital destiny of her daughter for years, then know that the battle against your marital destiny could be ferocious and dangerous. Unnecessary marital delays are caused by evil forces, family cum generational curses, and even initiation into evil cults. A sister, as a little kid was initiated into her family goddess cult, being the first born she was not meant to be married, but to grow up to serve the goddess as a shrine prophetess. It took a whole lot of deliverance services before she could be set free. Deliverance Ministers stormed her roots in the village to break those evil bondages.

Only through God that you can secure victory over the forces of the enemy. I decree in the name of Jesus that you shall leap over the wall of limitation. By God's grace and power you shall run through a troop and take delivery of your marital destiny.

No devil or his cohorts shall be able to hinder you any longer in Jesus mighty name! "For by thee I have run through a troop; and by my God have I leaped over a wall."(Psalms 18:29)

The quality of your relationship endeavors is a product of your faith. Faith is the instrument you need to quench all the fiery darts of the wicked that are shot against your marital destiny. The Bible says, "Above all, taking the shield of faith, wherewith ye shall be able to quench all the fiery darts of the wicked." (Eph 6:16)

In my book, "Getting what you want by Faith", I eloquently and profoundly postulated that in the kingdom of God, the most valuable currency is faith, and that our faith is a kind of currency that is accepted by God in exchange for whatever we want from Him. It's a known fact that the world uses dollars and other currencies in exchange for goods and services. In the kingdom of God it is faith we use to secure our desires from God!

Faith has power to secure your marital destiny.

Faith has power to give you the husband or wife of your choice.

Faith has power to change your marital status, from being a single to a married person.

You see, in this journey of life, lots of people know what they want out of life, but very few actually engage the power of faith to get what they want. Knowledge alone is not enough. Faith is a must for every single who seriously desires to secure a glorious marriage.

Lack of faith has made some single folks to miss the train of their marital destiny. Nothing happens in our world without faith. No single or intending suitor will get married outside of faith. If you don't want to remain a single for a long time, you must accept personal responsibility to work on your faith with a view to developing it. Jesus always said to many people that came to Him for one help or the other, "It shall be unto you according to your faith..."

Faith is a powerful key to open the door to your marital destiny. If you have faith that you too can get married and enjoy a blissful marriage, it shall be so with you!

What is faith?

In our context, Faith is your ability to have a firm, solid trust or confidence in the goodness and power of God to intervene in your marital destiny. Faith here is not about your confidence in your beauty, money or position! Your faith should not stand on your skill or abilities but in the power of God. Apostle Paul said, "And my speech and my preaching was not with enticing words of man's wisdom, but in demonstration of the Spirit and of power: That your faith should not stand in the wisdom of men, but in the power of God." (1 Corinthians 2:4-5)

It is the power of God that changes people's stories! Yours shall be changed too!

In Mathew 9:27-30, two blind men came to Jesus and asked Him to heal them. Jesus first asked them, "Do you believe that I am able to do this?" and their reply was, "Yes, LORD." Then He touched their eyes saying, "According to your faith let it be unto you."

Do you also believe God is able to settle you maritally? Not minding your generational or hereditary propensities for delayed or no marriage at all? As you're reading this book, I sincerely do believe that the Spirit of God is already doing a quick work in your marital destiny, you're being overshadowed, and the best in you is emerging, that evil covering is being removed right now! Shout a loud "Amen"!

Why is faith needed in your quest to securing your marital destiny?

Faith is needed to make an impossible marital case become possible. No impossibility can survive where faith is at work. "Jesus said unto him, If thou canst

believe, all things are possible to him that believeth."
(Mark 9:23)

Without faith it is impossible to overcome or gain
victory over the devil and his cohorts. Faith is needed
to secure victory over forces of the enemy. "For
whatsoever is born of God overcometh the world: and
this is the victory that overcometh the world, even our
faith." (1John 5:4)

And most importantly, without faith it is impossible
to please God! "But without faith it is impossible to
please him: for he that cometh to God must believe
that he is, and that he is a rewarder of them that
diligently seek him." (Hebrews 11:6)

If you please Him with your faith, He will please you
with your choice partner!

How to develop faith that delivers results

You can develop your faith by the word of God!
Because the word of God is the authentic source of
faith. The more of His word you take into your spirit
the more your faith develops. Locate a word from
scriptures that prohibits you from being single for a

long time unnecessarily. For instance, if you can take this word: "And the LORD God said, It is not good that the man should be alone; I will make him an help meet for him.", you will never remain single for long!

How can the one who made the male and female, not bless you with your own partner.

God who made them both male and female has a spouse for you!

God who said it is not good for Adam to be alone has a partner for you!

God who made it possible for Ruth, a widow to marry a rich bachelor, called Boaz, has a "Boaz" for you!

Contemporarily, God who made it possible for one of my beloved daughters in the Lord to settle down not minding her ugly past, will settle you too!

Faith is action! Faith cannot develop until it is acted upon. Until you put God's word into action, your faith will never develop. Faith comes by hearing and doing the word of God. Action is the only way to prove that you believe!

Say or Speak what you want by faith

In Mark 11:23, Jesus says, "... he shall have whatsoever he saith." In our context, whatever you "say" concerning your marital destiny will become a practical reality!

Do you believe God has a spouse for you? Then speak it into existence! Tell the whole world that you have a partner that will soon manifest. It is possible to talk with him, play with him, eat with him. Like I did when my wife and I were looking for the fruit of the womb. Read my book "Getting what you want by Faith" and get a full story of how I was eating with my potential son! The Bible says, "We having the same spirit of faith, according as it is written, I believed, and therefore have I spoken; we also believe, and therefore speak;" (2 Corinthians 4:13)

Take a step of faith now!

Yes, you can take a step of faith right now!

You can by faith set a date for your wedding, then proceed further to buy your wedding gown in preparation for your wedding!

I once instructed a beloved daughter of God to take her faith to the next level of "conceptualising and visualising" her husband by buying a shirt for him. That she should learn to talk with her husband via the shirt. She did it as instructed and later came back with a testimony of how God beautified her with a husband, whose shirt size was exactly the same with the shirt she had bought for her "imaginary" husband! Faith work can be crazy or unfathomable at times you know!

May I use this medium to also instruct you to buy a beautiful shirt, preferably a unisex, for your husband, which you too can wear. What do I do with the shirt, you may ask? Keep the shirt in your wardrobe or where you keep your own clothes. By faith always declare thus:

"My husband please come and wear your shirt."

"My husband can I wear your shirt today?

"My husband, your shirt is dirty can I help you wash it?

By so doing you live with the consciousness of a partner in your life. And God will honor your step of faith in Jesus' name!

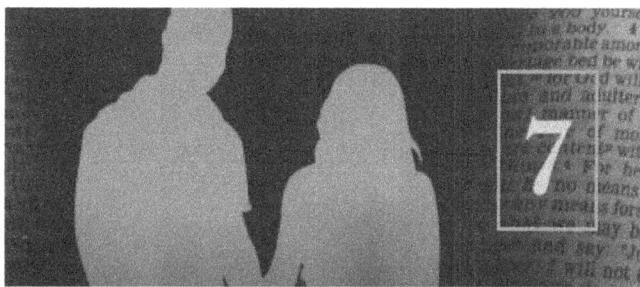

7 ENGAGING POWER INSTRUMENTS

You can not possess your marital destiny on a platter of gold. I don't mean to scare you! Possessing your possession is no cheap talk or wishful thinking, it is real fight. Nothing good comes easy! God gave the children of Israel the land of Canaan but not without a fight. "Behold, the LORD thy God hath set the land before thee: go up and possess it, as the LORD God of thy fathers hath said unto thee; fear not, neither be discouraged." (Deuteronomy 1:21)

You need to concertedly and proficiently engage power Instruments to secure your marital destiny, but before you engage these instruments, ask the Holy Spirit to show you the instrument that is apt and auspicious for your situation. You need a guided missile to target the enemy. Just one guided stone from David finished that giant - Goliath. Just one guided missile will finish the enemy of your marital destiny. May God arise and give you a "stone" to bring down the head of your enemy in the mighty name of Jesus.

Instrument of a Vow

A vow is a solemn pledge or promise to do a specified thing. Hannah vowed a vow, and said, "O LORD of hosts, if thou wilt indeed look on the affliction of thine handmaid, and remember me, and not forget thine handmaid, but wilt give unto thine handmaid a man child, then I will give him unto the LORD all the days of his life, and there shall no razor come upon his head." (1 Samuel 1:11)

Hannah engaged this instrument to get what she wanted - a male child! You too can engage the instrument of a vow to secure a spouse of your choice! Don't settle for less! Go for the best! Any vow that is targeted at advancing the kingdom of God will attract the attention and intervention of God. If you vow, for instance, that God should bless you with a spouse that would join hands with you in serving God and His kingdom, that vow will procure heaven's blessing.

Vow a vow which will cost you something precious!

You can vow that if God should give you a spouse of your choice, you will give Him your precious car or your three months salary.

I have always encouraged our youths and singles to ask God for specific blessings as they keep their covenant of purity COP – a public pledge of chastity. Every year at Camp Joseph, our annual youth leadership training conference, young people come out openly to vow to God that they would not engage in premarital sex until their wedding night.

Instrument of Angelic Intervention

Angelic hosts are powerful forces prepared by God to minister or serve you as an heir of salvation. The Bible says, "Are they not all ministering spirits, sent forth to minister for them who shall be heirs of salvation?" (Hebrews 1:14)

There is a place (partner) which God has prepared for you! "Behold, I send an Angel before thee, to keep thee in the way, and to bring thee into the place which I have prepared." (Ex 23:20)

There is a partner God has ordained for you!

There is a beautiful marriage for you.

I decree that your Angel will intervene in your life with a view to helping you fulfill your marital destiny.

Just as David engaged his angel against his enemies, you too can do same. David decreed:

"... and let the angel of the LORD chase them. Let their way be dark and slippery: and let the angel of the LORD persecute them." (Ps 35:5-6)

You too can decree that your angel should chase strange women out of your prospective husband's life. And also that your angel should persecute all those frustrating your marriage dreams and plans.

Whatever prison the devil has shut you up in, I decree your freedom by angelic intervention right now! Just as Daniel was thrown into the den of lions but the Lord sent His angels to deliver him, you too shall be free. In the book of Acts, we read of Peter being locked up in prison. While the saints of God prayed, an angel went into the prison and set him free. "And, behold, the angel of the Lord came upon him, and a light shined in the prison: and he smote Peter on the side, and raised him up, saying, Arise up quickly. And his chains fell off from his hands." (Acts 12:7)

You are a child of destiny. You have a glorious marriage and a colorful home. But there are many enemies! The devil is all out to contest your glorious marriage. Apostle Paul said, "For a great door and effectual is opened unto me, and there are many adversaries." (1Cor 16:9)

Arise and release your angels! Order your angel to take action according to your marital desires. Invoke the name of Jesus to trigger off your angel. Boldly declare: "In the name of Jesus, my angel I mandate you right now to go and fetch my husband for me from wherever he may be. My angel cause my path to cross my God ordained spouse's path within 21 days. Go fast and bring my partner to me. Open my partner's eyes to see me. Make it easy for my partner to find me."

It is godly to pray that your angel should blind your partner's eyes from seeing the wrong person. And that your angel should frustrate and stop every wrong relationship your God ordained partner may be engaged in. If you have faith, and you truly engage your angel, you shall have a tearful testimony within 21 days!

Instrument of the blood of Jesus

"And the blood shall be to you for a token upon the houses where ye are: and when I see the blood, I will pass over you, and the plague shall not be upon you to destroy you, when I smite the land of Egypt." (Exodus 12:13)

Every plague ravaging your marital destiny can be arrested and defeated by the blood of Jesus! If the blood of bulls and goats could be used to set the children of Israel free from bondage, then be rest assured that you too shall secure your freedom from every enemy of your blissful marriage. The Bible says, "In whom we have redemption through his blood, the forgiveness of sins, according to the riches of his grace;" (Ephesians 1:7)

If the blood of Jesus is that powerful to secure your redemption or salvation, then there is nothing the blood cannot secure for you.

Getting a befitting partner to marry is no big deal or a big task for the blood of Jesus to handle. I see the blood of the Lamb drawing you near to your prospective partner!

By faith, I hereby use the blood of Jesus to purge you from every sin or iniquity that has stood on your path to securing your marital destiny. The Bible says, "And almost all things are by the law purged with blood ..." (Hebrews 9:22)

By the blood of Jesus Christ that speaks better things than the blood of Abel, I purge you from your past mistakes, failures, and disappointments! You are now washed and purged to commence a robust relationship!

Instrument of a sent Word

The Bible says, "He sent his word, and healed them, and delivered them from their destructions." (Psalm 107:20)

A word from the Lord is all you need to secure your marital destiny. You must pray for a sent word.

Be hypersensitive to catch a word from the altar or from your personal word study as you concertedly go on a search. The word is your final authority on any issue of life, and your marital issue is not excluded. Kenneth Copeland said, "If you will make the Word the final authority in your life, it will give you stability when everything else around you gives way. If you'll let what God says settle the issues of life, you will be confident when others are confused, you will be at peace when others are under pressure, you will be overcoming when others are being overcome!"

What does it mean to make the Word your final authority? It means believing what God says instead of believing what man says. It means believing what God says instead of what Satan and his cohorts say.

It means believing what the Word says instead of what your background or circumstances say.

Make up your mind to live by the Word!

Instrument of a prophetic ministry

A true prophet or man of God is sent to wipe away your tears. Through him your marital destiny can be secured. "And by a prophet the Lord brought Israel out Egypt, and by a prophet was he preserved." (Hosea 12:13)

Your marital prosperity is tied to the man of God you believe in as your pastor or prophet. The Bible says, "... believe in the Lord your God, so shall ye be established; believe his prophets, so shall ye prosper." (2Chro. 20:20)

Do you have a pastor or prophet in your life who speaks into your life? Do you believe in his ministry? Then he can be used of God to deliver you from delayed or late marriage. Ask him to pray and declare some marriage-inducing blessings into your life. With all sense of modesty and responsibility, I am one of the God sent prophets to youth and singles of my generation. God has validated my ministry to singles with credible proofs. My father in ministry, Bishop David Oyedepo said, "only fools doubt proofs!" Countless number of singles have been delivered from delayed marriage via my ministry. You shall not be an exemption! Only believe!

Please accept these declarations by faith:

I decree and declare that your hour of settlement is now! I proclaim Favour of God upon you! His Favour shall cause you to be chosen like Esther.

I decree and declare that your God ordained partner shall locate you within 21 days!

I decree and declare that the wickedness of the wicked shall come to an end in your life, even as God Himself will arise to fight against them that fight against you in the name of Jesus. Amen!

Instrument of the Anointing

The anointing is designed by God to destroy yokes of the devil in your life! The Bible says, "And it shall come to pass in that day, that his burden shall be taken away from off thy shoulder, and his yoke from off thy neck, and the yoke shall be destroyed because of the anointing." (Isaiah 10:27)

I don't care about the yoke of delay that the enemy has placed around your neck, all I care about is the fact that God's anointing is powerful enough to shatter and scatter such yokes forthwith! Only believe! Now anoint your forehead with anointing oil and declare thus: "By this anointing I break off every yoke of delay from my life in Jesus' name" Do this often as you are led by the Holy Spirit!

The anointing is such a powerful instrument, such that after David was anointed by God's servant, Samuel, his fame was proclaimed or announced in the palace by one of the king's servants, which I describe as the "next level" facilitator. What was the effect of this proclamation? David was invited to the palace! The Bible says, "Then answered one of the servants, and said, Behold, I have seen a son of Jesse the Bethlehemite, that is cunning in playing, and a mighty valiant man, and a man of war, and prudent in matters, and a comely person, and the LORD is with him. Wherefore Saul sent messengers unto Jesse, and said, Send me David thy son, which is with the sheep." (1Samuel 16:18-19)

I believe also that the anointing could cause you to be announced in right quarters, and you shall be connected to your God ordained "palace" - spouse! Now anoint your forehead with anointing oil and declare thus: "By this anointing, I'm being announced and introduced to my lovely partner in Jesus' name!"

My beloved single, do you realize that delayed or no marriage at all could be a kind of social or emotional sickness? I know a single lady who was looking so emaciated as if she was sick in her body, but when she got married, she became so "well" that everybody was surprised. Her "sickness" was social and emotional. The anointing of God is designed to handle all kinds of sickness! Be it physical! Be it emotional! The Bible says, "Is any sick among you? let him call for the elders of the church; and let them pray over him anointing him with oil in the name of the Lord." (James 5:14)

There is nothing wrong in asking your pastor or elders in your church to pray and anoint you with oil in the name of Lord with a view to securing your marital destiny. Every morning you too can personally anoint your forehead and declare God's word over your life. In the kingdom of God, self-deliverance is permitted. Remember that David encouraged himself in the Lord when he was at his lowest ebb, as such you too can anoint yourself in the name of the Lord. Now anoint your forehead with anointing oil and declare thus: "I'm delivered from every social or emotional sickness of delayed marriage forthwith in Jesus' name! I'm getting married to my God ordained partner in Jesus' name! My hour of blissful marriage is finally here. Glory to God!"

If you have been impacted or blessed by this inspirational book please feel free to pass it on to someone. Also feel free to contact me for any personal or exclusive prayers! I'm expectant of your testimony!

Please share with me!

joejesimiel2006@yahoo.com

01-2934286, 08023124455

Appendix

My Second Chance

I grew up in a Christian home where my parents and siblings attended church regularly. I volunteered in the children's ushering department since I was about 11 years old. I had the knowledge of God and I believed in Him and I longed to have a closer relationship but I could not commit the time to studying His word and praying to Him regularly. In my final year in school, a friend invited me to YDI and I started attending after school. At that time a lot of kids spoke about different youth clubs and it was almost like an in thing to belong to a youth club just for the sake of belonging and probably meeting people. Knowing myself, I was not good at making friends so I had never bothered despite several invitations from different people to different youth clubs.

My entrance into Young Disciples International (YDI) started opening my eyes to see things differently about the God I have heard so much about. I started to understand the relationship that could be formed with a friend whom I had thought as an imaginary greater being we had to give honour to for our existence. I began to understand His love for me and the sacrifice that was made for me to have access to speak with Him the way I could now do.

The thing is, even though we learnt a lot of things from Pastor Joe and other youth workers, the influence and encouragement I received were from teenagers just like me. It was a positive peer pressure. At YDI, I could talk about God freely and be proud to be a Christian without someone calling me an 'SU' (a term that was used derogatorily to describe a religious student who talked about God). If I did not have a good day at school, I could always look forward to a good time at YDI where there was no class, no race, no discrimination of any sort.

My grooming time in YDI gave me access to commit my life to Christ anew and I entered a covenant of purity with God. The strength and power I had in me made it easy to make this decision. However, not long after I had to go to school in South Africa where I was faced with a different challenge. Without a support group, I quickly found myself drifting and again being influenced by the need to be loved and accepted, I became far from God.

I went away from what I had learnt from YDI but I was not far from it. I still remembered there was a God that loves me much more that I could imagine. Every time I found myself in a dark spot I always remembered to call on Him and He always heard me. My desire to get to that point where I have a very strong relationship with God never left me and eventually influenced me to marry a so-called Christian. Everything seemed fine at the beginning.

But sooner my sweet life began to turn sour. I started to wonder if God was punishing me for failing on my covenant of purity. Then I called Pastor Joe whom I had been hiding or running away from just because I was not the better Christian I had longed to be, and told him what I was going through. Pastor Joe was there for me, reminding me of God's love for me. He spoke to me about God making things work for my good even if I had made wrong choices. I went back home with the objective of being a better Christian. It seemed easy as I felt I was obeying God's commandment but was still not at the point I wanted to be in my relationship with God.

My first marriage was hitting the Rock, before I knew it my then husband wanted me out of his house. He frustrated every effort I did to save our marriage to the point I started thinking of taking an "easy" but permanent way out of my problems. Several counseling did not help. It only made me feel worse as almost everyone had to link my husband's behavior to something they thought I had done. I hit rock bottom and felt God had deserted me but somehow a still small voice still reminded me of God's love for me. I was not alone. God raised help from people that would usually not lift their hands to help me. I decided to leave my marriage as I strongly believed that God would prefer me alive than dead just because I did not believe in divorce. In all, my God was never too far from me and my pastor, Pastor Joe was always a phone call away.

God gave me a second chance. It was like I was never married before. All the years, time and effort I spent in my first marriage which seemed like a waste of my time was given back to me like it never happened. His word promises me He would rebuild the years that the cankerworm and caterpillar has stolen, and He did just that. I thought I had lost everything but I gained it all back. My life experiences have taught me that we are not all equal and we all cannot be the same. We can however all desire to have a long lasting relationship with God and as we journey on an unknown terrain, He makes an exit for us every time we take a wrong turn. He sees our hearts and hears our innermost thought so He understands most when no one else understands what you are going through. He communicates with us through His word and if we are not listening or reading or paying attention,

He sends help our way to point us in the right direction.

Truly, God is a God of second chance! He is ever faithful!

Mrs Faith Boegheim

A YDI Associate, and professional Pilot.

OTHER BOOKS BY THE AUTHOR

Building an Effective youth Ministry

Becoming Rich and wealthy

Get Motivated! Who says you can't make it?

Hebrew Women's Style

How to Obtain Favour from God and Man

Young but Mighty

Essentials of Career Choice

The youth God Uses

Understanding Courtship and Premarital Issues

Questions that Singles Ask - Vol.1

Strategies for Stress free Relationships

Can Boys and Girls also go to Hell?

Child Neglect: Is the Church Guilty?

Teenagers and Relationships

Youth and Friendship

Youth and opportunity

Striving for Excellence

Enjoying God's Mercy

Getting What you Want by Faith

www.ingramcontent.com/pod-product-compliance
Lightning Source LLC
Chambersburg PA
CBHW071907020426
42331CB00010B/2706